Celebrating
Kwanzaa

By: Julie Williams
Illustrated by: Marie-Claude Monchaux

Published by Abdo & Daughters, 4940 Viking Drive, Suite 622, Edina, Minnesota 55435.

Copyright © 1996 by Abdo Consulting Group, Inc., Pentagon Tower, P.O. Box 36036, Minneapolis, Minnesota 55435 USA. International copyrights reserved in all countries. No part of this book may be reproduced in any form without written permission from the publisher.

Printed in the United States.

Illustrations by Marie-Claude Monchaux.

Edited by Julie Berg

Library of Congress Cataloging-in-Publication Data

Williams, Julie.
    Kwanzaa / Julie Williams.
        p. cm. -- (Holiday celebrations)
    Summary: Explains in rhyming text the customs associated with the African-American harvest holiday Kwanzaa.
    ISBN 1-56239-707-9
    1. Kwanzaa--Juvenile literature. [1.Kwanzaa.] I. Title.
II. Series: Holiday celebrations (Edina, MN.)
GT4403.W55 1996
394.2'61--dc20   96-13026
                                                            CIP
                                                             AC

Celebrating
Kwanzaa

Marie-Claude Monchaux

HARVEST HOLIDAY

Our holiday has seven letters:
K-W-A-N-Z-A-A.
It has seven symbols,
teaches seven values—
one for each weekday.

We celebrate the harvest
each day a new candle is lit.
The last night the family gathers
for food, stories, and gifts.

UMOJA

(oo-MOH-jah)

Dad and I wear our dashikis;
he says, "No blue jeans!"
Mom puts on her busuti
and looks like an African queen.

We set the table with our mkeka mat
and the kinara made by Uncle James;
with seven candles, black, red and green
it's called the "keeper of the flames."

Next we set out two ears of corn,
symbolizing Jojo and me.
Mom says Umoja stands for unity
of our family and community.

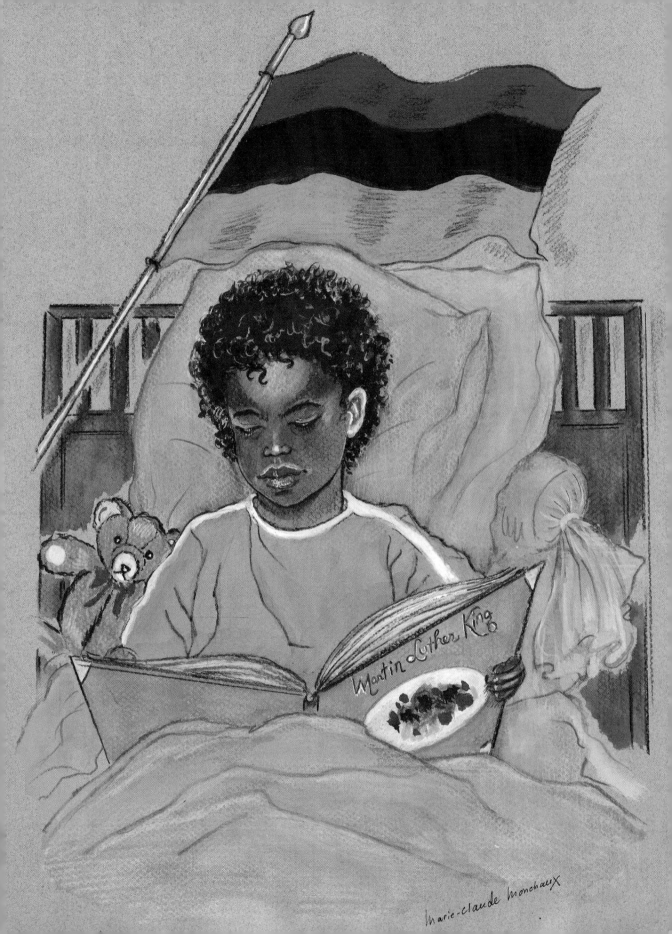

marie-claude monchaux

KUJICHAGULIA

(KOO-gee-CHA-goo-LEE)

Black, green, and red
is the flag above my bed.
Black is for our people,
red, for the struggles that life brings.
Green stands for the color of hope.
On this second day we remember
Kujichagulia means "do the right thing."

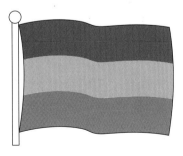

UJIMA

(oo-GEE-mah)

Maya's washing, I'm drying,
Dad is shoveling the walk.
Mom's on her computer
and Grandmother starts to talk:

"On this third day of Kwanzaa
we are doing as we should.
We must always help each other—
which honors all sisters and brothers."

UJAMAA

(oo-jah-MAH)

Plink!
Plunk!
Plank!
Coins fall into my bank.

I'm saving for a bicycle
and Kwanzaa gifts for my brothers.
Ujamaa reminds us to save our money,
but to also share with others.

marie Claude michaux

UJAMAA MARKET

On the fourth day of Kwanzaa
my father takes us all
to the Ujamaa Market,
set up in a big hall.

Drummers, dancers, singers
perform throughout the night;
merchants selling all their goods—
it's such an awesome sight!

NIA

(NEE-ah)

On the fifth night,
Nia,
a green candle burns bright
to honor our ancestors
who stood up for what was right.

KUUMBA

(koo-OOM-bah)

When Maurice hits his bells
called an African agogo,
you can hear two different notes—
one sounds high, the other low.

Frankie beats the conga drums.
I do a basket dance.
Kuumba celebrates creativity, and
each person gets a chance.

FESTIVAL OF FOODS

Fried chicken,
corn bread,
sweet potato pie,
collard greens,
catfish,
and peas that are called black-eyed.

Aunt Keesha's peach cobbler,
and sweet corn—so many ears.
Never again will I eat so much...
'til we celebrate next year!

IMANI

(ee-MON-ee)

Imani means faith,
so we must stand and be strong.
We must believe in our future
and celebrate with songs.

People's faith survived slavery.
It strives for justice and equality—
so all the world can live in peace,
love, and harmony!

marie-Claude monchaux

GIFTS OF LOVE

Zawadi are what we call the gifts
to improve our minds and hearts:
history tales, hand-strung beads,
or books of African art.

Homemade or store-bought,
it doesn't really matter.
Besides, Mom says her best gift
was the kiss and hug I gave her!

A HISTORY
OF
BLACK
AMERICA

marie-claude monchaux

KWANZAA KARAMU

(kah-RAH-moo)

Harambee!
Habari gani!
We stand and greet at the door
our uncles, aunts and cousins
arriving with food, presents, and more.

We'll sing, dance, and storytell
and open our gifts—at last!
Great-grandmother passes the unity cup
to honor our family of the past.

THE NGUZO SABA
(The seven principles of Kwanzaa)
by Maulana Karenga

1-UMOJA

(Unity)

To strive for and maintain unity in the family, community, nation, and race.

2-KUJICHAGULIA

(Self-determination)

To define ourselves, name ourselves, create for ourselves, and speak for ourselves instead of being defined, named, created for, and spoken for by others.

3-UJIMA

(Collective Work and Responsibility)

To build and maintain our community together and make our sisters' and brothers' problems our problems and to solve them together.

4-UJAMAA

(Cooperative Economics)

To build and maintain our own shops, stores, and other businesses and to profit from them together.

5-NIA

(Purpose)

To make our collective vocation the building and developing of our community in order to restore our people to their traditional greatness.

6-KUUMBA

(Creativity)

To do always as much as we can, in the way we can, in order to leave our community more beautiful and beneficial than we inherited it.

7-IMANI

(Faith)

To believe with all our heart in our people, our parents, our teachers, our leaders, and the righteousness and victory of our struggle.

GLOSSARY

DASHIKI (da-SHE-kee) brightly-colored, loose-fitting, pullover garment.

KIKOMBE CHA UMOJA (kee-KOM-bay CHA oo-MOH-jah) is the unity cup. It is used to pour a libation (ly-BAY-shun), called "tambiko" (tam-BEE-koh), in honor of the ancestors. These ancestors are all the people who have come before us, including such African Americans as Harriet Tubman and Martin Luther King, Jr. They are also the enslaved Africans who struggled to survive, to raise their families, and to build a new life of freedom. When people drink from the simple wooden cup, they honor all the people who lived before them. The cup is a symbol of unity.

KINARA (kee-NAH-rah) is the candleholder with places for seven candles. It should be simple and is often handmade. The kinara is a symbol for the African people who are the ancestors of African Americans.

MAZAO (mah-ZAH-oh) are the fruits and vegetables of the harvest. As in the early days of African history, farmers still work together to raise crops for food. The harvest is a time of joy and thanksgiving. Having a bountiful harvest shows that the farmers have cooperated and are successful. The mazao, the fruits of the harvest, stand for the origins of Kwanzaa.

MISHUMAA SABA (mee-shu-MAH SAH-bah) are the seven candles of Kwanzaa. They represent the seven principles, the Nguzo Saba. There is one black candle, three red candles, and three green ones. On each night of Kwanzaa, a new candle is lit until on the last day, they are all kindled together. The black candle is in the center, with the red candles to the left and green candles to the right.

MKEKA (em-KAY-kah) is the mat on which all the other symbols rest. Often it is woven out of grasses. Some people use mats made in Africa, but many others weave their own out of fabric or strips of paper. The mkeka is a symbol of tradition and history.

MUHINDI (moo-HIN-dee) are ears of dry corn, one for each child living in the household. Some people have an extra ear of corn to symbolize unborn generations. The ears of corn are the "fruit" of the cornstalk. The ears represent the dream of parents that their own children and future generations will grow strong.

ZAWADI (zah-WAH-dee) are the Kwanzaa gifts that parents give to their children. By having lived according to the Kwanzaa values during the year, the children can now "reap" the harvest of their work. Parents like to give educational games and books, or special handmade gifts. In this way, even the zawadi can help reinforce the values of Kwanzaa.